Stella Maidment and Lorena Robe

G000293121

Happy Street

Activity Book

2

OXFORD
UNIVERSITY PRESS

OXFORD
UNIVERSITY PRESS

Great Clarendon Street, Oxford OX2 6DP

Oxford University Press is a department of the University of Oxford. It furthers the University's objective of excellence in research, scholarship, and education by publishing worldwide in

Oxford New York

Athens Auckland Bangkok Bogotá Buenos Aires Calcutta
Cape Town Chennai Dar es Salaam Delhi Florence
Hong Kong Istanbul Karachi Kuala Lumpur Madrid
Melbourne Mexico City Mumbai Nairobi Paris São Paulo
Shanghai Singapore Taipei Tokyo Toronto Warsaw

with associated companies in Berlin Ibadan

Oxford and Oxford English are registered trade marks of Oxford University Press in the UK and in certain other countries

ISBN 0 19 433842 8

Printed and bound in Spain by Book Print S.L., Barcelona

Acknowledgements
The authors and publishers would like to thank all the teachers who have contributed so usefully to the project at all stages of its development.

Designed by: Amanda Hockin

Illustrations
Happy Street characters and artwork by Peter Stevenson
Quizzy and Ziggy characters and artwork by Bernice Lum

Kathy Baxendale pp 8, 15, 16, 26, 36, 42, 43, 46, 56, 66, 76, 79, 86; Phil Dobson pp 17, 19, 23, 27, 37, 47, 52, 54, 55, 57, 62, 63, 67, 77, 80, 84, 85, 87; Martin Faulkner p 80; Teri Gower pp 4, 19, 22, 24, 25, 32, 35, 40, 44, 45, 60, 70, 73

Commissioned photography by: Haddon Davies

The publishers would like to thank the following for permission to reproduce photographs:
Environmental Images p 70 (Cornwall/Daphne Christelis, rain/Graham Burns); Oxford Scientific Films p 70 (storm clouds/Marty Cordano)

1 **Read and draw.**

2 **Solve the puzzle and write.**

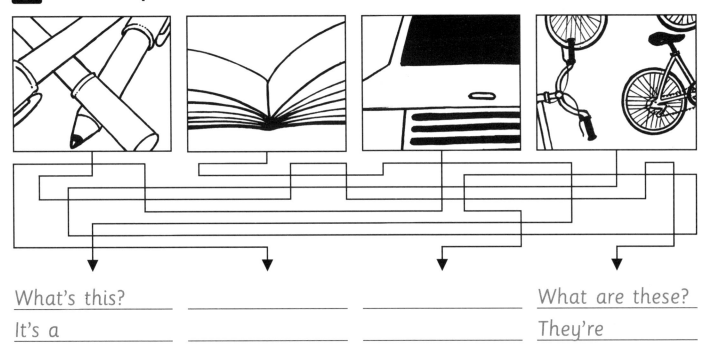

What's this?

It's a

What are these?

They're

1 ⌐4⌐ **Listen and circle.**

1. A (F) Z
2. T O W
3. S R B
4. C H U
5. I P K
6. E L Y

2 **Play Alphabet Bingo.**

3 **Choose and write.**

What's this?
They're letters too! Look – 'Z' and 'Z'!
And this is a cake – for you!

It's a letter 'Q'.
And what are these, Ziggy?

1

What's this?

2

3

4

1 🔢6 Listen and number.

2 Read and colour.

Red = all the things beginning with 'c'.   Purple = all the things beginning with 's'.

Yellow = all the things beginning with 'b'.   Green = all the things beginning with 'd'.

3 Solve the puzzle. Follow the instructions.

a	b	c	d	e	f	g	h	i	j	k	l	m	n	o	p	q	r	s	t	u	v	w	x	y	z
☆	●	△	▨	■	◆	◗	○	▼	★	▩	◐	▲	◖	◇	■	▽	✮	▲	▢	◉	◆	▽	▢	◈	◖

1   ▽✮▽▢■ ◈◇●✮ ◖☆▲■ ◇◖ ▢○■ △☆▨■.

‾‾‾ ‾ ‾ ‾ ‾   ‾ ‾ ‾ ‾   ‾ ‾ ‾ ‾   ‾ ‾   ‾ ‾ ‾   ‾ ‾ ‾ ‾.

2   ▨★☆▽ ☆ ■◐✮◖◐■ ◇◖ ▢○■ ▢-▲○▼✮★▢.

‾ ‾ ‾ ‾ ‾   ‾   ‾ ‾ ‾ ‾ ‾ ‾   ‾ ‾   ‾ ‾ ‾   ‾ ‾-‾ ‾ ‾ ‾ ‾.

3   △◇◐○◇●✮ ▢○■ ●▼▨■ ✮■▨.

‾ ‾ ‾ ‾ ‾ ‾ ‾   ‾ ‾ ‾   ‾ ‾ ‾ ‾   ‾ ‾ ‾.

4 Write a message in code for your friend.

1 🔊8 **Listen, write, and draw.**

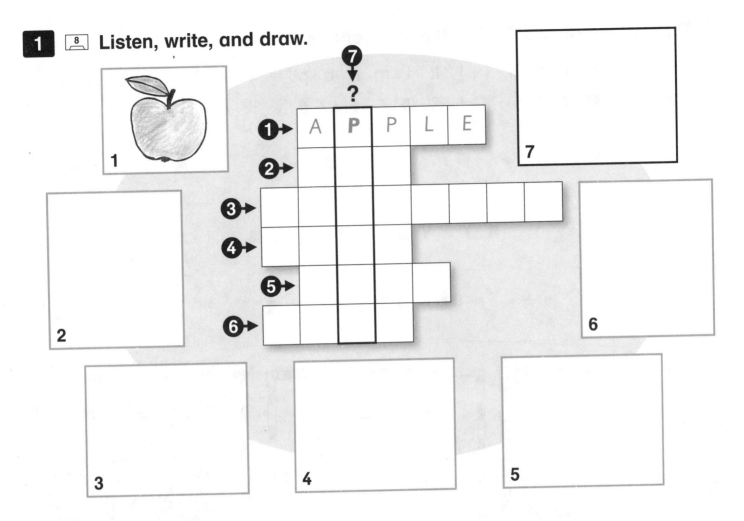

2 **Read and write.**

bo _____

ca _____

bo _____

bi _____

or _____

di _____

② Happy families

1 🔟 **Colour, then listen and match.**

1 = yellow   2 = red   3 = blue   4 = green   5 = black

2 **Write sentences with *his* or *her*.**

It's her cat.

It's

They're

It's his

1 🔊 11 **Listen and number.**

2 **Choose and write.**

mum   dad   brother   sister   grandpa   grandma   uncle   auntie   cousin

1 She's Polly's _sister._

2 He's Polly's _____

3 He's Polly's _____

4 She's Polly's _____

5 He's Polly's _____

6 She's Polly's _____

7 He's Polly's _____

8 _____'s Polly's _____

9 _____'s Polly's _____

3 **Choose and write.**

Hello, Tizzy.   And this is her sister, Tizzy.   Fizzy?

No, his name's Fred!   Ziggy, this is my cousin, Lizzy.

Hello, Lizzy!   And this is her brother...

1

Ziggy, this is my cousin, Lizzy.

2

3

4

1 🔊14 **Listen and colour.**

1	2	3	4	5	6	7	8	9	10
11	12	13	14	15	16	17	18	19	20
21	22	23	24	25	26	27	28	29	30
31	32	33	34	35	36	37	38	39	40
41	42	43	44	45	46	47	48	49	50
51	52	53	54	55	56	57	58	59	60
61	62	63	64	65	66	67	68	69	70
71	72	73	74	75	76	77	78	79	80
81	82	83	84	85	86	87	88	89	90
91	92	93	94	95	96	97	98	99	100

2 **Match, then write the names.**

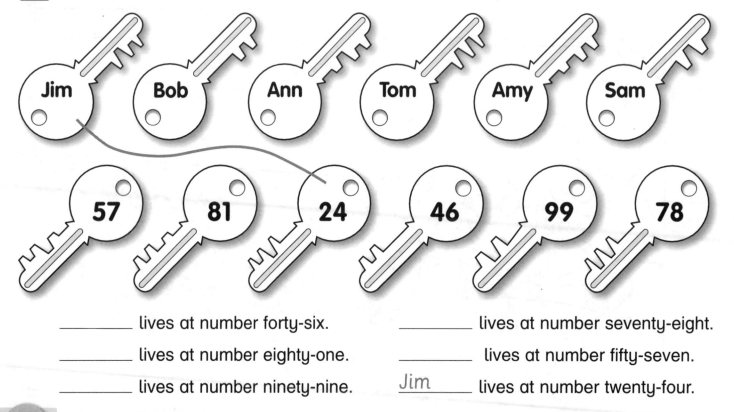

Jim   Bob   Ann   Tom   Amy   Sam

57   81   24   46   99   78

_____ lives at number forty-six.

_____ lives at number eighty-one.

_____ lives at number ninety-nine.

_____ lives at number seventy-eight.

_____ lives at number fifty-seven.

Jim lives at number twenty-four.

3 **Read and join.**

1 My dad's mum is my   uncle.

2 My mum's dad is my   auntie.

3 My dad's brother is my   grandma.

4 My cousin's mum is my   grandpa.

4 **Write.**

Greg Dawson
12 Happy Street
Happy Town
England

I live at number 12 Happy Street with my mum, my dog, and her three puppies!

I live at number _____

_____, with my

_____

_____

1 ⌨ 16 **Listen and write the numbers. Then write the names.**

1

Ben

brothers [2]

sisters [1]

2

Emily

brothers [ ]

sisters [ ]

3

James

brothers [ ]

sisters [ ]

4

Rosie

brothers [ ]

sisters [ ]

_____ hasn't got any brothers or sisters.

_Ben_____ has got two brothers and one sister.

_____ has got one sister.

_____ has got three brothers.

2 **Read, colour, and write.**

Otto's got two brothers and one sister. They are Samson, Sid, and Millie. One is black, one is brown, and one is grey. One brother lives at number thirty-two. He isn't black. His name is Samson. Otto's sister is grey. She lives at number forty-seven. Her name is Millie. Otto's black brother lives at number fifty-eight. What is his name?

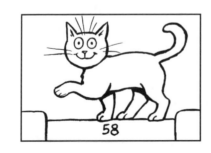

This is Otto's brother.

His name is _Samson_____.

He is _____.

He lives at number 32.

This is Otto's _____.

_____ name is _____.

_____ is grey.

_____ lives at number _____.

This is _____.

_____

_____

_____

14

3 **Ask your friends.**

Name	Brothers	Sisters
● Ziggy	1	1
● Ming	0	0
●		
●		
●		
●		
●		

How many brothers and sisters have you got?

4 **Write about your friends.**

Ziggy has got one brother and one sister.

Ming hasn't got any brothers or sisters.

1 **Choose and write.**

brown   His   She's   twelve   sister   eyes   little

This is me, my brother, and my
_____sister_____ .
My _____ brother is four
years old. _____ name is
Robbie. He's got blond hair and
blue _____ .
My sister is _____ years old.
Her name is Lucy. _____ got
_____ hair and blue eyes,
just like me!

2 **Draw and write.**

About ME!

This is me and my _____
_____
_____
_____
_____
_____
_____
_____

3 🔊 **17** **Listen and repeat. Then write the words in the Sound Machine.**

lives   big   bike   fifty   nine   six   five   white

six

nine

4 🔊 **18** **Listen and check with the Sound Machine.**

RHYME TIME

5 🔊 **19** **Say the rhyme.**

His bike, her bike, your bike, my bike,
Black bikes, white bikes, big and small.
Everybody here's got different bikes.
But I like MY bike best of all.

Quizzy's Questions

Can you say these family words?

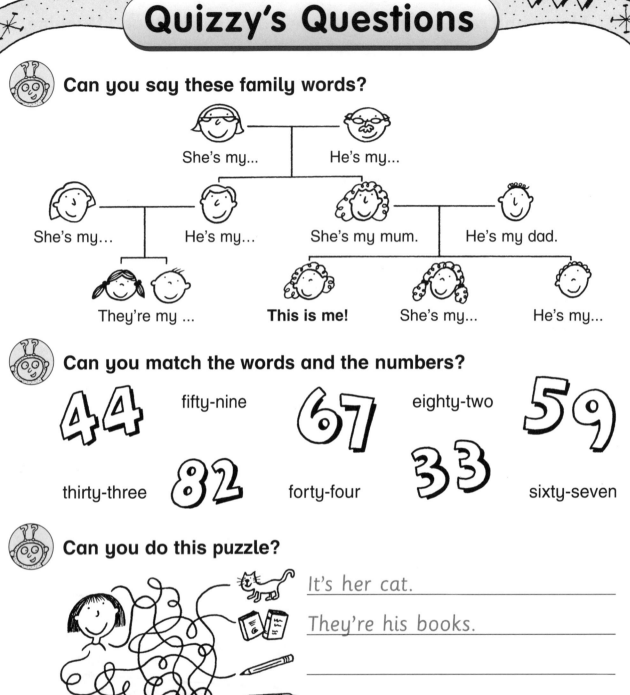

She's my... He's my...

She's my... He's my... She's my mum. He's my dad.

They're my ... **This is me!** She's my... He's my...

Can you match the words and the numbers?

44   fifty-nine   67   eighty-two   59

thirty-three   82   forty-four   33   sixty-seven

Can you do this puzzle?

It's her cat.

They're his books.

_____

_____

_____

Now think about your progress.

OK ◯   Good ◯   Excellent ◯

18

3 Food, food, food!

1 📻 22 **Listen and put a ✓ (likes) or a ✗ (doesn't like).**

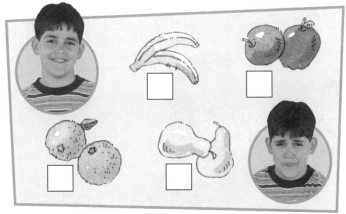

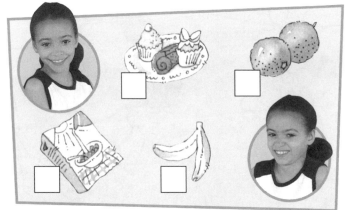

2 **Choose and write.**

| bananas | ice cream | cake | oranges | apples | pears |

1 He likes _apples_ .

2 She doesn't like _____ .

3 She _____ .

4 He _____ .

5 _____ .

6 _____ .

1 🔊 23 **What's in the shopping bag? Listen and circle.**

2 **Choose and write.**

> bread any some she any got some milk cheese eggs

Polly's got some _____s_ and she's got _____ rice. She's got some _____ but _____ hasn't got _____ bread.

Jack hasn't got _____ eggs or rice. He's _____ some _b_____, some _____, and _____ grapes.

3 **Choose and write.**

No, I don't. Yuck!   Mmm! Yum! Grapes!   Oh, Quizzy!

And he doesn't like eggs.   Quizzy doesn't like cheese.

But he likes grapes.   Eggs! Yuck! No, I don't.

1 📻 26 **Listen and number.**

2 **Read and draw.**

1   It's four o'clock.

2   It's one o'clock.

3   It's half past nine.

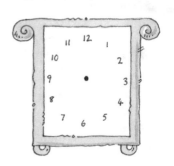

4   It's seven o'clock.

5   It's half past five.

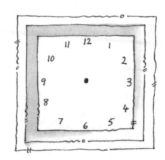

6   It's half past three.

3 **Look, then complete the sentences.**

I have breakfast at _____ .   I have breakfast at _____ .

I have lunch at _____ .   I have lunch at _____ .

I have dinner at _____ .   I have dinner at _____ .

4 **Draw and write.**

I have breakfast at _____   I have lunch at _____   I have dinner at _____

_____ .   _____ .   _____ .

1 Read dialogue 1. Then complete dialogues 2 and 3.

1

Can I have an orange juice, please?

Anything else?

No, thank you.

Here you are. An apple juice.

No! Not an **apple** juice – an **orange** juice!

Sorry!

2

Can I have a large lemonade, please?

_____?

No, thank you.

_____.
_____
_____!

No! Not a **small** lemonade – a **large** lemonade!

_____!

3

_____
cheese _____,
_____?

Anything else?

____, _____.

Here you are. An egg sandwich!

____! _____
_____ –
_____
_____!

Sorry!

2 Write a menu.

cafe

Food

_____
_____
_____
_____

Drinks

_____
_____
_____
_____

3 👥 Now act out a dialogue with a friend.

Can I have a large orange juice, please?

Anything else?

1 Write *sometimes, always* or *never*. Then ask a friend.

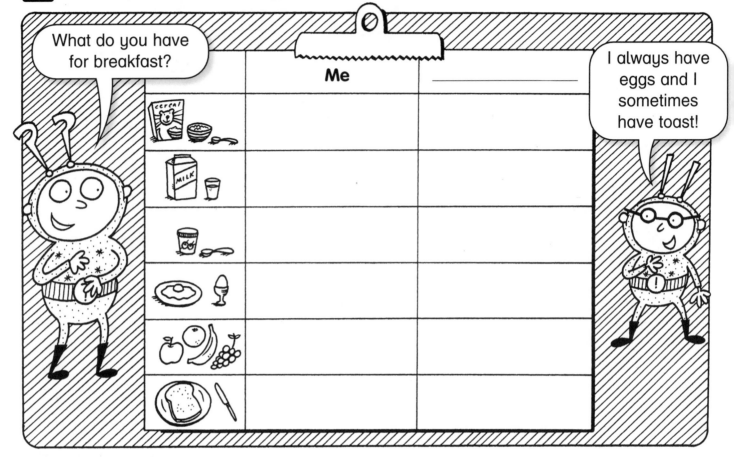

2 Now write about you and your friend.

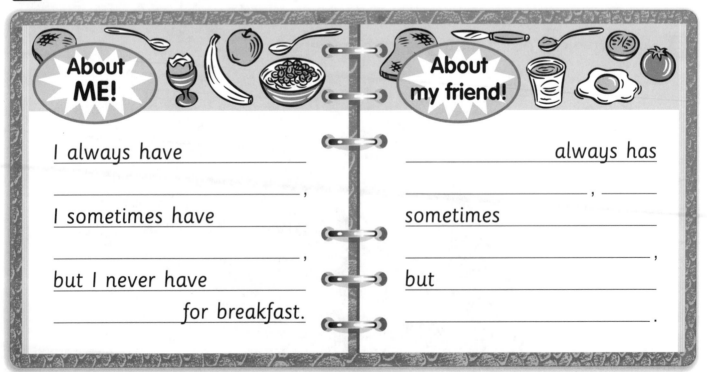

About ME!

I always have _____, _____
I sometimes have _____, _____
but I never have _____ for breakfast.

About my friend!

_____ always has _____, _____
sometimes _____, _____
but _____.

3 🔊 28 **Listen and repeat. Then write the words in the Sound Machine.**

gate   any   eight   breakfast
grapes   bread   cake   egg

egg

cake

4 🔊 29 **Listen and check with the Sound Machine.**

RHYME TIME

5 🔊 30 **Say the rhyme.**

Eggs and bread, then ten red grapes
With seven cakes on a plate,
Every day at half past eight
We have breakfast – don't be late!

Quizzy's Questions

 Can you say these times? Put a ✓ or a ✗.

 Can you do this puzzle?

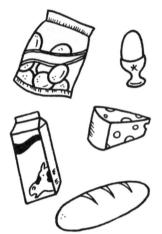

```
X  L  B  H  M  B  E  L  C
D  P  U  C  R  I  S  P  S
R  A  E  T  P  S  L  G  G
K  S  I  G  V  C  R  K  B
E  T  O  S  G  U  I  J  R
S  A  N  D  W  I  C  H  E
F  Y  N  R  M  T  E  W  A
A  C  H  E  E  S  E  T  D
G  R  A  P  E  S  R  I  C
```

 Can you write sentences?

1 got He's some biscuits   <u>He's got some biscuits.</u>

2 any crisps hasn't got She   _____

3 apples doesn't He like green   _____

4 o'clock lunch She one at has   _____

    _____

5 for sometimes cereal has breakfast She   _____

    _____

6 never He sandwiches lunch for has   _____

    _____

Now think about your progress.

OK ◯   Good ◯   Excellent ◯

4 A day at the zoo

1 🔊 36 **Listen and circle *Yes* or *No*.**

1 Yes No   2 Yes No   3 Yes No

4 Yes No   5 Yes No   6 Yes No

2 **Write.**

1
They aren't friendly.
They're dangerous.
They aren't funny.

2
_____ friendly.
_____ dangerous.
_____ funny.

3
_____
_____
_____

4
_____
_____
_____

1 38 **Listen and draw the route.**

2 **Read and write.**

monkey   lion   penguin   elephant   hippo   snake

1 It's in picture B and picture C. It isn't in picture A.   It's <u>an elephant</u>.

2 It's in picture A and picture B. It isn't in picture C.   It's <u>a </u>.

3 It's in picture A and picture C. It isn't in picture B.   It's _____.

4 It's in picture A, picture B, and picture C.   It's _____.

5 It's in picture A. It isn't in picture B or picture C.   It's _____.

6 It's in picture B. It isn't in picture A or picture C.   It's _____.

3 Choose and write.

Hello, Quizzy!

No! They're lions! Aagh!

No, they aren't lions. They're boys!

Look! Are they lions?

1 Look! Are they lions?

2

1 📼 40 **Listen and circle *Yes* or *No*.**

1 Yes No

2 Yes No

3 Yes No

4 Yes No

5 Yes No

6 Yes No

2 **Read, write the names, and colour.**

Jill is wearing a blue T-shirt. She's taller than Jenny.
Jenny is wearing a red T-shirt. She's fatter than Jill.
Molly is wearing a yellow T-shirt. She's younger
and shorter than Jenny and Jill.

3 **Make sentences about the animals.**

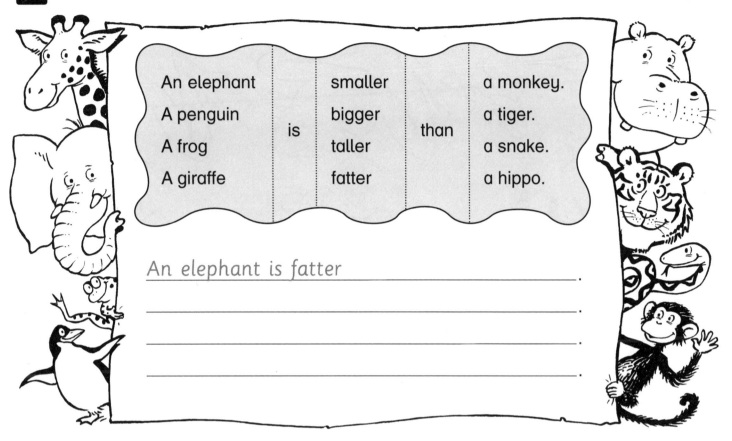

An elephant		smaller		a monkey.
A penguin	is	bigger	than	a tiger.
A frog		taller		a snake.
A giraffe		fatter		a hippo.

An elephant is fatter _____ .

_____ .

_____ .

_____ .

4 **Read. Then write about you and your friend.**

I'm younger than Amy and I'm taller than Amy.

I'm _____

_____ .

1 ⌷42⌷ **Listen and colour.**

2 **Read and write.**

In the zoo there are lots of animals. The hippos are between the elephants and the giraffes. The parrots are opposite the shop and next to the tigers. The tigers are between the penguins and the parrots. The monkeys are opposite the tigers. The toilets are between the cafe and the lions.

3 **Draw the animals. Then write about your zoo.**

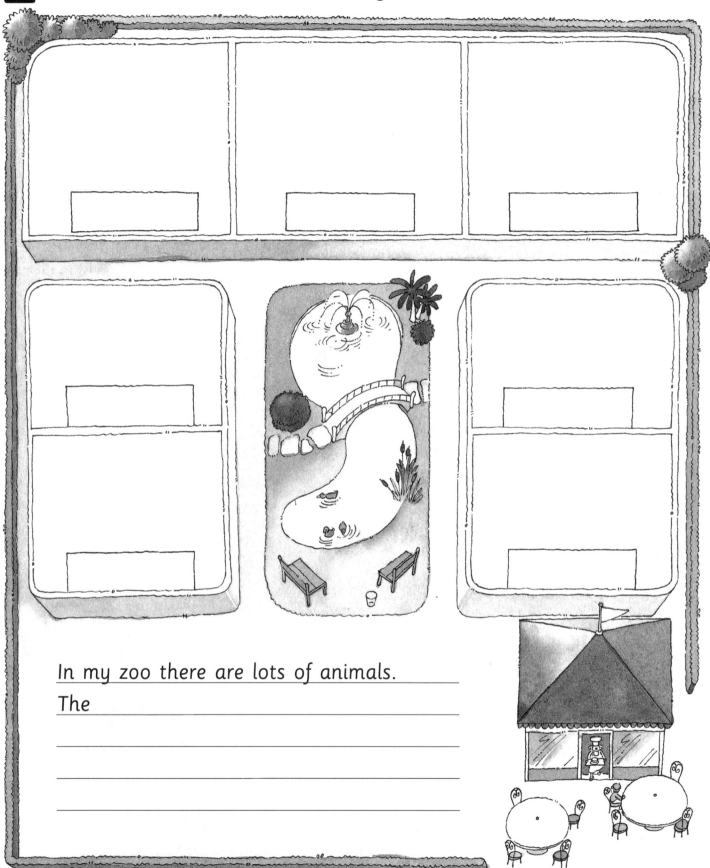

In my zoo there are lots of animals.
The

1 **Read Polly's poem.**

Tigers, tigers,
Beautiful tigers!
Tigers, tigers,
Dangerous tigers!
Tigers, tigers,
Strong tigers!

... I love tigers!

2 **Write a poem about an animal you love.**

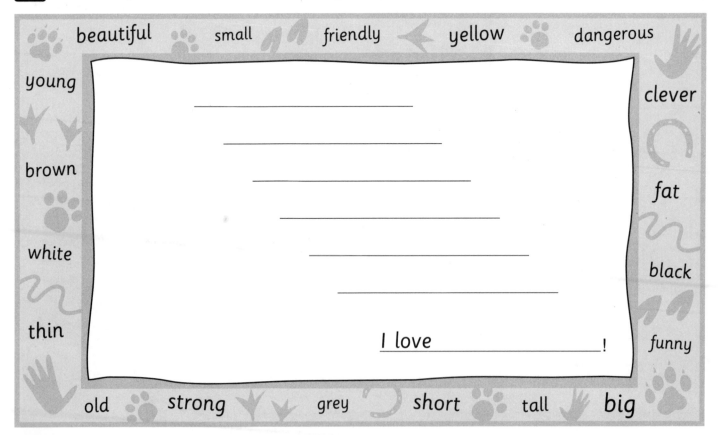

beautiful   small   friendly   yellow   dangerous

young

clever

brown

fat

white

black

thin

I love _____ !

funny

old   strong   grey   short   tall   big

3 🔊 43 **Listen and repeat. Then write the words in the Sound Machine.**

bigger   dangerous   giraffe   grey   large   tiger   orange   bag

bag

orange

4 🔊 44 **Listen and check with the Sound Machine.**

RHYME TIME

5 🔊 45 **Say the rhyme.**

My giraffe likes orange juice
In a very big glass with a straw.
But my tiger likes grape juice, in a mug.
He always growls for more. Grrr!

Quizzy's Questions

 Can you talk about these animals?

bigger   fatter   smaller   taller

 Can you do this puzzle?

There are eight children in the picture. Pat is opposite Sam. Jan is between Sam and Sue. Sue is opposite Tim. Dan is between Sue and Pat. Flo is between Tim and Sam.

Where is Ben?

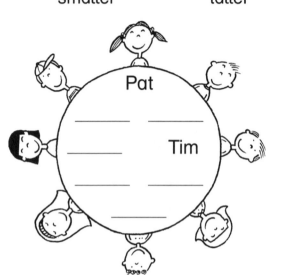

 Can you write about these animals? Use these words:
funny fat dangerous brown big thin grey small

 Lions are brown. They aren't grey.

 _____

  _____

 _____

Now think about your progress.

OK ◯   Good ◯   Excellent ◯

5 In the town

1 Read, look, and circle A or B.

1 There's a plane.   (A)   B   4 There aren't any dolls.   A   B

2 There are two kites.   A   B   5 There isn't a small dinosaur.   A   B

3 There's a boat.   A   B   6 There are lots of balls.   A   B

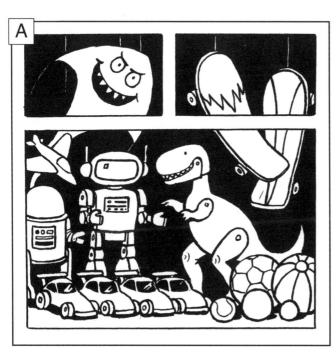

2 Write about your classroom.

In my classroom there's a
_____ .

There isn't a _____ .

There are lots of _____ .

There aren't any _____ !

1 📻 **49** **Listen and write.**

cafe   library   toy shop   restaurant   church   supermarket

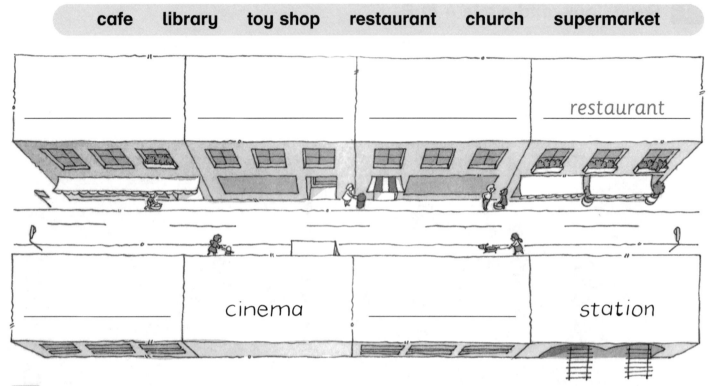

_____ _____ _____ restaurant

_____ cinema _____ station

2 **Look and write.**

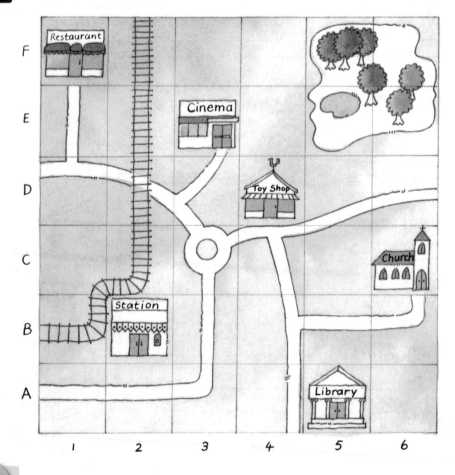

B2 = the station

D4 = _____

F1 = _____

E3 = _____

C6 = _____

A5 = _____

3 **Choose and write.**

> Look! There's a beautiful church! Quizzy? Quizzy?

> And there are lots of shops! I'm here, Ziggy. In the restaurant.

Look! There's a beautiful church!

1 🔊51 **Listen and circle.**

2 **Read and answer. Then complete the graph.**

In my class there are twenty-eight children. There are fifteen boys and thirteen girls. Five boys and seven girls go to school by car, three boys and two girls go to school by bus, and two girls and three boys go to school by bike. How many children walk to school?

_____ boys and _____ girls walk to school.

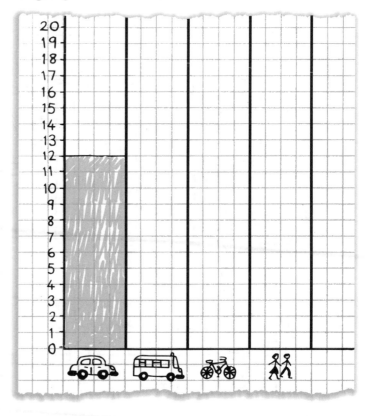

42

3 **Do a class survey. Ask your friends and write their names.**

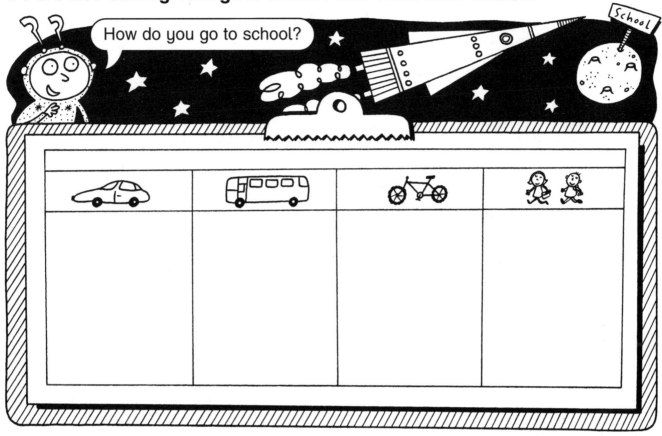

How do you go to school?

4 **Draw a graph and write about your class.**

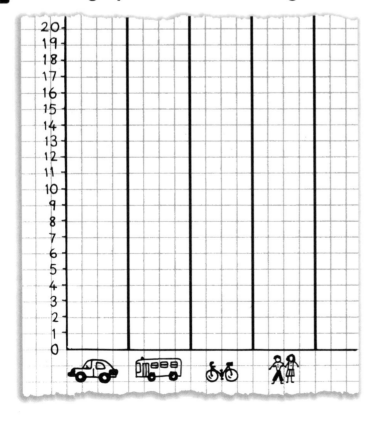

In my class there are _____

_____ children.

_____ children

go to school by car.

_____

_____

_____

_____

_____

_____

1 📻 53 **Listen and match.**

65p   80p   50p   95p   70p   30p

2 **Find and write the words.**

  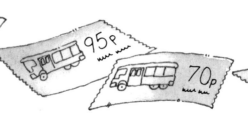 

cinema

```
s p o r t s c e n t r e
c q n e v t h q w e y f
h d o s i z u j h b n g
o u b t f t r v b n m c
o r k a l s  c i n e m a
l z b u e v h o r t u f
l i b r a r y m j f p e
y s t a t i o n k g o t
e w q n x s h o p y u g
a o t t l o f d a t n h
s v b n z q p b r w z j
s u p e r m a r k e t k
```

3 Match.

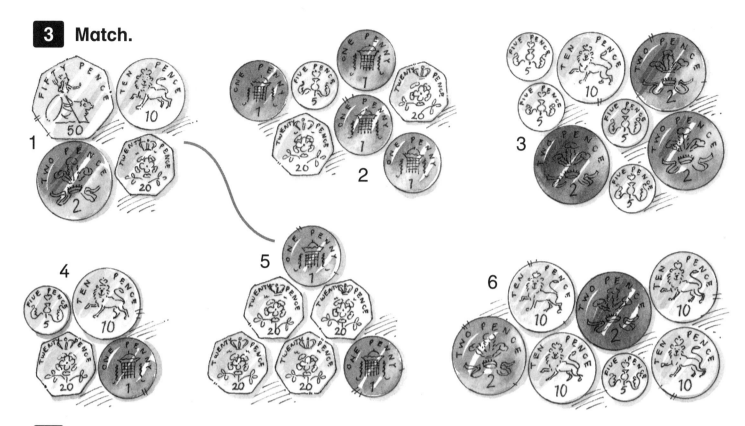

4 Read dialogue 1. Then complete dialogues 2 and 3.

1

 The school, please.

That's 75p.

 How much?

75p.

 Here you are.

Thank you.

2

The library, please.

_____ 65p.

How much?

_____

Here you are.

_____

3

_____
_____

That's 90p.

_____?

90p.

_____

Thank you.

1 Choose and write.

> are   shops   there   small   any   isn't

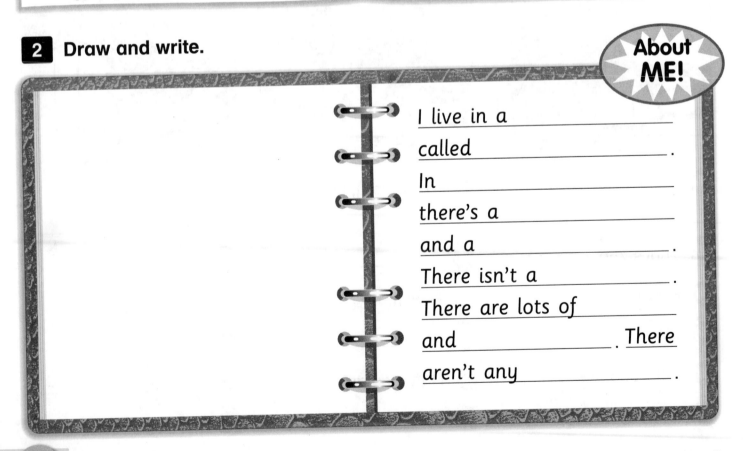

I live in a _____ town called Newbridge. In Newbridge there _____ lots of houses and _____. There's a school, a sports centre, a cafe, two restaurants, and a big park. There _____ a station and _____ aren't _____ cinemas. I like my town!

2 Draw and write.

About ME!

I live in a _____
called _____.
In _____
there's a _____
and a _____.
There isn't a _____.
There are lots of _____
and _____. There
aren't any _____.

3 🔊 54 **Listen and repeat. Then write the words in the Sound Machine.**

banana   black   can't   half   taxi
     cafe   van   car

taxi

car

4 🔊 55 **Listen and check with the Sound Machine.**

RHYME TIME

5 🔊 56 **Say the rhyme.**

Quick! Call a taxi! Quick as you can!
My auntie's car has a flat front tyre!
Quick! Call a fire engine! Quick as you can!
Help! My dad's black van's on fire!

Quizzy's Questions

Can you say these words? Put a ✓ or a ✗.

Can you complete the speech bubbles?

1 — I _____ to school _____ .

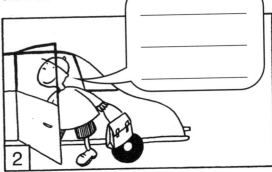

2

3

4

Can you make sentences?

Look! There's	any vans in the car park.
There isn't	a fire engine next to the cinema!
There are	a restaurant in the church.
There aren't	some big shops in the shopping centre.

Now think about your progress.

OK ◯   Good ◯   Excellent ◯

48

1 📻 **59** **Listen and draw.**

2 **Choose and write.**

like	going
don't like	playing
	swimming
	watching

1 I _like watching_ television.

2 I _____ to the supermarket.

3 I _____ .

4 I _____ football.

1 🔊60 **Listen and number.**

2 **Read and write.**

I love playing with my friends Mo, Holly, and Amy, but they all like doing different things! Mo's nine and she likes going to the sports centre. She loves playing basketball. Amy and Holly are ten. They like going to the sports centre but they don't like playing basketball. Mo and Holly really like dancing, but Amy doesn't – she likes swimming. Amy, Mo, and Holly like going to the cafe. There are some computer games in the cafe and Amy and Holly like playing computer games... but Mo doesn't!

Name ___Mo___
Age __9__
Likes
going to the sports
centre,
_____
_____
_____

Doesn't like
_____
_____

Name ___Holly___
Age ____
Likes
_____
_____
_____
_____

Doesn't like
_____
_____

Name _____
Age ____
Likes
_____
_____
_____
_____

Doesn't like
_____
_____

50

3 **Choose and write.**

No, I don't.   Do you like rollerblading?   No, I don't.

Here you are, Ziggy.   Do you like running, Quizzy?

Erm... thank you.   But we always have dinner at six o'clock!

1 — Do you like running, Quizzy?

1 🔲62 **Listen and write the days of the week.**

4 M	8
5	9
6	10
7	

2 **Read and write.**

I go _swimming_ on _Mondays_.
I play _____ on _____.
I _____ shopping on _____.
I watch _____ on _____.
I _____ my bike on _____.
I _____ judo on _____.
I do my _____ on _____.

_ r _ _ _ _ y

_ _ d _ _ _ _ d _ _ _

_ a _ _ r _ _ _ _

S _ n _ _ _ _

M o n d a y

_ u _ s _ _ _ _

T _ _ r _ _ a _

3 **Read and write.**

On Mondays and Fridays I play football in the park – it's great fun. On Tuesdays I go swimming with my brothers. On Wednesdays I go to the supermarket with Mum – I don't like Wednesdays! On Thursdays and Sundays I do my homework and watch television. Saturday is my favourite day! On Saturdays I go to the sports centre – I love playing basketball.

Monday	*play football*
Tuesday	
Wednesday	
Thursday	
Friday	*play football*
Saturday	
Sunday	

4 **Choose and write.**

Monday	go swimming
Tuesday	do my homework
Wednesday	have a piano lesson
Thursday	play basketball
Friday	do judo
Saturday	go to my dad's cafe
Sunday	do my homework watch TV

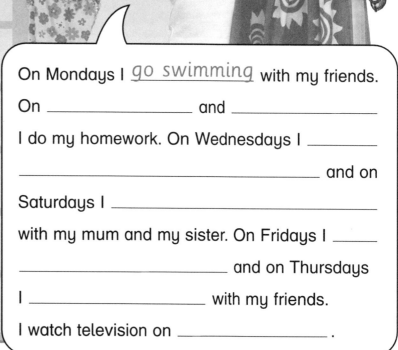

On Mondays I _go swimming_ with my friends. On _____ and _____ I do my homework. On Wednesdays I _____ _____ and on Saturdays I _____ with my mum and my sister. On Fridays I _____ _____ and on Thursdays I _____ with my friends. I watch television on _____.

1 🔊 65 **Listen and match.**

2 **Write the names of television programmes in your country.**

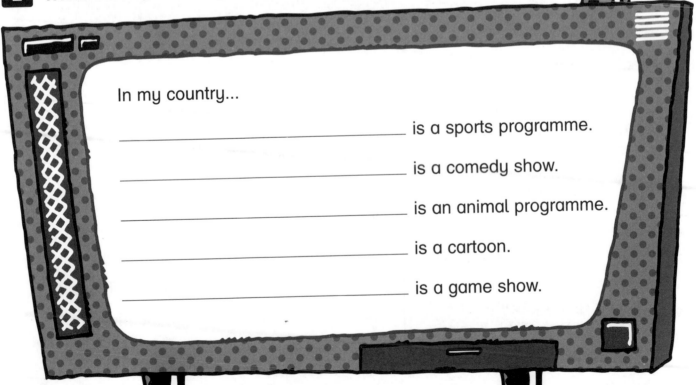

In my country...

_____ is a sports programme.

_____ is a comedy show.

_____ is an animal programme.

_____ is a cartoon.

_____ is a game show.

3 Write about the television programmes in Activity 2.

I always watch _____

_____ .

I sometimes watch _____

_____ .

I never watch _____

_____ .

4 Write about you and your family.

I like watching _____ and _____ but I don't like

watching _____ or _____ . My favourite

programme is _____ .

My _____ likes watching _____ and _____

_____ but _____ doesn't like watching _____ .

_____ favourite programme is _____ .

My _____ likes watching _____ and _____

_____ but _____ doesn't like watching _____ .

_____ favourite programme is _____ .

_____

_____

1 **Choose and write.**

half past five   Channel   watch   favourite   3   Wednesdays
game show   programme   always

My _____ programme is 'Tom and Jerry'.
It's a cartoon. It's on _____ at four o'clock
on _____ 2. I _____ watch it.

My favourite _____ is '3-2-1-Go!' It's a
children's _____ . It's on Mondays and
Thursdays at _____ on
Channel _____ . I always _____ it.

2 **Draw and write.**

My favourite programme is
_____ .
It's _____
_____ .
It's on _____
at _____
on Channel _____ .

3 [66] **Listen and repeat. Then write the words in the Sound Machine.**

cartoon   rice   comedy   cinema   cereal   cake
juice   cafe

cake

cereal

4 [67] **Listen and check with the Sound Machine.**

RHYME TIME

5 [68] **Say the rhyme.**

My cousin's on a cookery show
With cake all over his face!
There's orange juice all over the floor
And rice all over the place!

Quizzy's Questions

 Can you talk about these children?

✓ = likes...   ✗ = doesn't like ...

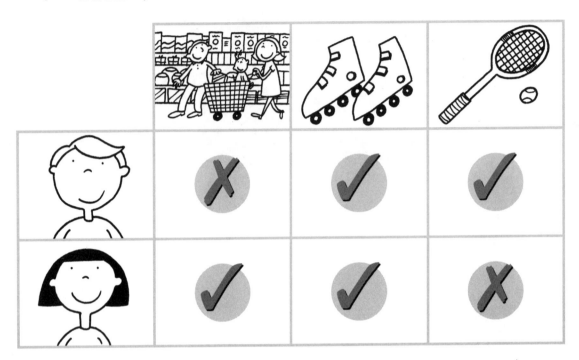

 Can you say the days of the week?

Monday...

 Can you make sentences?

On Mondays I play	my favourite cartoon.
On Thursdays I watch	swimming lessons.
On Fridays I have	my homework.
On Sundays I do	football.

Now think about your progress.

OK ◯   Good ◯   Excellent ◯

58

7 People at work

1 74 **Listen, number, and match.**

2 **Choose and write.**

go   quarter past   have   half past   have   get up   quarter to

I _____ at seven o'clock.

I _____ a shower at seven.

I _____ breakfast at eight, and at eight

I _____ to school.

1 🔊 75 **Listen and number.**

2 **Write the words and number the pictures.**

firefighter   nurse   teacher   mechanic   office worker   baker

3 **Choose and write.**

Oh, yes. I always mend my car.   Thank you, Ziggy!   Help!
Are you a good mechanic, Quizzy?   And I'm a great firefighter!

1 Are you a good mechanic, Quizzy?

1 ⌷77 **Listen and number.**

2 **Read and write:** *Henry* **or** *Annette*.

This is Henry.

This is Annette.

1 _____ works in a restaurant.

2 _____ doesn't work in the town.

3 _____ makes lunch and dinner for people.

4 _____ doesn't work with animals.

5 _____ doesn't wear a big white hat.

6 _____ doesn't work at home.

3 **Read and write.**

| He / She | works / wears / drives | a bus. / in a library. / in a school. / a train. / a uniform. / in a restaurant. |

He
She

works
wears
drives

a bus.
in a library.
in a school.
a train.
a uniform.
in a restaurant.

1 _She works in a_
library.

2 _____

3 _____

4 _____
_____

5 _____
_____

6 _____
_____

1 📻 79 **Listen and circle A or B.**

1 A B
2 A B
3 A B
4 A B
5 A B
6 A B
7 A B
8 A B

2 **Read and write.**

This is Tina. She lives next to the school. Tina loves crisps – she always has a packet in her school bag. Tina likes books and playing tennis. She doesn't like watching television but she loves going to the cinema. Is it Tina's bag?

This is David. David goes to school by car with his dad. He likes playing computer games. He sometimes watches television but he never goes to the cinema. He likes books and he loves football. Is it David's bag?

This is Amanda. She loves films and books. She watches lots of television and loves going to the cinema, too. She likes playing computer games with her friends. She always brings crisps to school! Is it Amanda's bag?

Whose bag is this?

It's _____'s.

3 **Match and write.**

Polly always — tennis on Fridays.

She likes — cereal and toast for breakfast.

She doesn't — watching television.

She has — her favourite programme on Saturdays.

She plays — walks to school.

She watches — like playing computer games.

Polly always walks to school.

_____

_____

_____

_____

_____

4 **Invent a friend for Quizzy and Ziggy. Draw and write.**

_____ always _____

_____ .

_____ likes _____

_____ .

_____ doesn't like _____

_____ .

_____ has _____

_____

for breakfast, lunch, and dinner!

_____ plays _____ .

_____ watches _____ on television.

1 **Choose and write.**

have   ride   Sundays   swimming   homework

watch   bed   play

On _____ I _____ a big breakfast! In the morning I go _____ with Mum at the sports centre. After lunch I go to the park and I _____ my bike. Sometimes I _____ football with my friends. In the evening I do my _____. Then I _____ my favourite programme on television. I go to _____ at eight o'clock.

2 **Draw and write about your favourite day.**

About ME!

On _____

I _____

_____

_____

_____

_____

_____

_____

3 〔80〕 **Listen and repeat. Then write the words in the Sound Machine.**

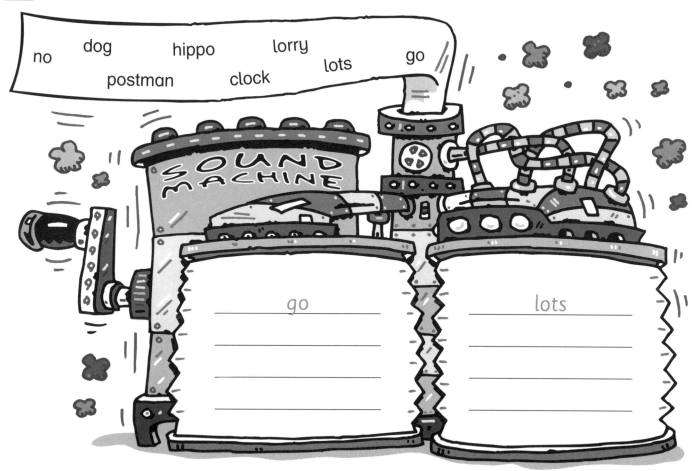

no   dog   hippo   lorry   go
postman   clock   lots

go

lots

4 〔81〕 **Listen and check with the Sound Machine.**

RHYME TIME

5 〔82〕 **Say the rhyme.**

I've got a hippo, but nobody knows.
My hippo's going in a lorry to the show.
He's a clever hippo – he's top in the show.
He isn't a dog! Shhh! But nobody knows!

Quizzy's Questions

Can you draw these times?

  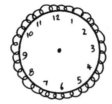 

quarter past two   six o'clock   half past five   quarter to seven

Can you talk about your day? Put a ✓ or a ✗.

 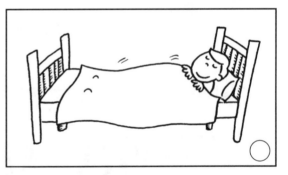

Can you make sentences?

I'm a baker and I	doesn't walk	a fire engine.
He's an astronaut and he	drives	a computer.
I'm an office worker and I	don't work	to work every day.
She's a firefighter and she	use	in an office.

Now think about your progress.

OK ◯   Good ◯   Excellent ◯

What's the weather like?

1 🔲85 **Listen and circle *Yes* or *No*.**

1 Yes No 2 Yes No 3 Yes No

4 Yes No 5 Yes No 6 Yes No

2 **Choose and write.**

making playing listening reading talking watching

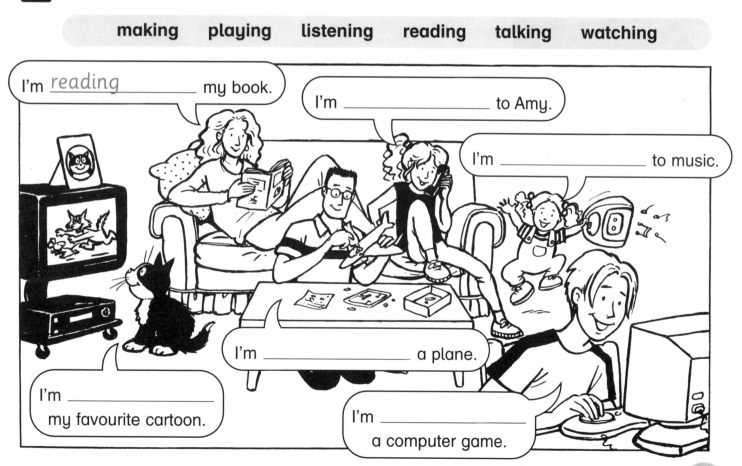

I'm *reading* _____ my book.

I'm _____ to Amy.

I'm _____ to music.

I'm _____ a plane.

I'm _____ my favourite cartoon.

I'm _____ a computer game.

1 ☐87 **Listen and number.**

2 **Read and match.**

It's hot and sunny.

It's raining.

It's snowing.

It's foggy.

It's cloudy.

70

3 Choose and write.

Look, Ziggy, I'm making a snowman!

It's too hot today!

Yes, it's an ICE CREAM snowman!

Mmm, yum!

But it's hot and sunny!

Hi, Quizzy!

1 🔊 89 **Listen and circle A, B, C or D.**

1 A B C D

2 A B C D

3 A B C D

4 A B C D

2 **Read, write, and colour.**

It's snowing and it's very cold today.

_____'s wearing an orange jumper, brown trousers, a brown and orange scarf, and black boots.

_____'s wearing a pink coat, a pink and white hat, pink trousers, and pink boots. She's got a pink umbrella too!

_____'s wearing a green coat, blue jeans, green boots, a black hat, and brown gloves.

_____'s wearing a purple and yellow hat, a blue coat, blue boots, purple trousers, and a purple and yellow scarf.

3 Find and write the words.

 ___hat___

t	r	o	u	s	e	r	s	p
x	j	u	m	p	e	r	f	g
z	p	z	b	i	s	l	c	l
y	r	c	r	h	a	t	o	o
r	b	g	e	f	y	s	a	v
n	o	j	l	s	t	h	t	e
m	o	l	l	k	b	o	v	s
c	t	r	a	i	n	e	r	s
q	s	c	a	r	f	s	j	g
h	k	u	j	t	w	e	k	h

 _____

 _____

_____

 _____

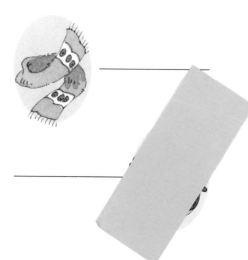 _____

_____

_____

_____

4 Draw and write.

1 It's _____ and

_____ .

I'm wearing _____

_____

_____

2 It's _____

_____

_____

_____

_____

1 Read and write A or B.

1 [A] It's sunny.

2 [ ] Grandpa is reading.

3 [ ] Polly is rollerblading.

4 [ ] Polly is playing tennis.

5 [ ] Uncle Tim is playing tennis with Jack.

6 [ ] Grandma is making a kite.

7 [ ] Bertie is watching Uncle Tim and Jack.

8 [ ] Daisy is wearing a hat.

2 **Write.**

What's Polly doing?
She's reading.
_____

What's _____ ?

He's watching television.

What's Greg doing?
_____
_____

_____ ?

She's swimming.

What's Dad doing?
_____
_____

_____ ?

She's playing the piano.

3 **Read and answer.**

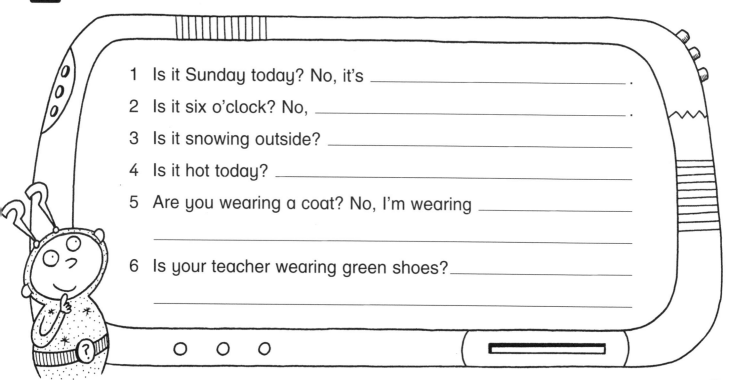

1 Is it Sunday today? No, it's _____ .

2 Is it six o'clock? No, _____ .

3 Is it snowing outside? _____

4 Is it hot today? _____

5 Are you wearing a coat? No, I'm wearing _____
_____

6 Is your teacher wearing green shoes? _____
_____

1 **Choose and write.**

scary   dad   big   boat   o'clock   dark
working   is   windy   torch   coming

I'm in a ____boat____ with my
friend Tom and his _____.
It's great! It's hot and sunny.

It's cloudy now and very
_____. Oh, no! The boat
isn't _____!

This is very _____. It's
nine _____ now. It's very
_____ and we haven't got
a _____.

Hooray - there's a _____
boat! It's _____ this way!
The man _____ waving!
We're safe!

2 🔊 **91** **Listen and repeat. Then write the words in the Sound Machine.**

food   book   cookery   cartoon
boots   look   zoo   good

good

zoo

3 🔊 **92** **Listen and check with the Sound Machine.**

RHYME TIME

4 🔊 **93** **Say the rhyme.**

What is that book? Can I have a look?
It's a very good book of cartoons – it's true.
But I need a book that's a cookery book,
So I cook food that's good for me and for you.

Quizzy's Questions

 Can you talk about the weather? Put a ✓ or a ✗.

 Can you colour the pictures and complete the sentences?

He's
wearing
_____ trousers,
a _____ jumper,
a _____ coat,
a _____ hat,
and _____
boots.

_____'s
_____
a _____ skirt,
a _____ jumper,
_____ shoes,
and _____'s got
a _____
umbrella.

 Can you write about these pictures?

_____ _____ _____

_____ _____ _____

Now think about your progress.

OK ◯   Good ◯   Excellent ◯

9 What happened?

1 [96] **Turn your book upside down and look at the picture. Then listen and circle *Yes* or *No*.**

1	Yes	No	3	Yes	No	5	Yes	No
2	Yes	No	4	Yes	No	6	Yes	No

2 **Look at Jack's diary, then choose and write.**

Monday _____
5.00: Swimming lesson at the sports centre
Tuesday _____
4.00: Cinema with Greg

Wednesday _____
3.30: Football match at school

Thursday _____
3.15: Supermarket with Mum

Friday _____
3.45: Sam's birthday party

Saturday _____
Morning: Remember library books!
Afternoon: Midford Castle with Dad
Sunday _____
Afternoon: Zoo with Grandma and Grandpa

> **was   wasn't   were   weren't**

1 Jack _was_____ at school at half past three on Wednesday.

2 Grandma and Grandpa _____ at the zoo on Saturday afternoon.

3 Jack _____ at school at five o'clock on Monday.

4 Jack _____ at Sam's birthday party on Friday.

5 Jack _____ at the library on Thursday.

6 Jack and Greg _____ at the cinema on Tuesday.

1 🎧 97 **Listen and circle A, B or C.**

| 1 | A | B | C | | 3 | A | B | C | | 5 | A | B | C |
| 2 | A | B | C | | 4 | A | B | C | | 6 | A | B | C |

2 **Read and match.**

Lady Lucinda Bates lived   lots of dogs.

She had   tennis with her friends.

She rode   dancing.

She played   in a big house.

She liked   her horse every day.

3 **Choose and write.**

Ha, ha! You had a funny little doll!

Look, Ziggy! This was me when I was three!

No, silly! That was my sister!

I lived in this house.

1 **Read and draw Quizzy's route.**

Quizzy's Saturday

On Saturday Quizzy had breakfast at home. After breakfast he went to the park and played football with Ziggy. For lunch they went to Pippo's pizza restaurant. Ziggy loves pizzas with lots of cheese, but Quizzy doesn't, so he had a steak and chips!

After lunch they said goodbye and Quizzy went to the cinema and saw a film. After the film Quizzy had an ice cream from the cafe opposite the cinema. Then he went to the toy shop and bought a new yo-yo.
At five o'clock he went home. It was a busy day!

2 🔊 **Listen and match.**

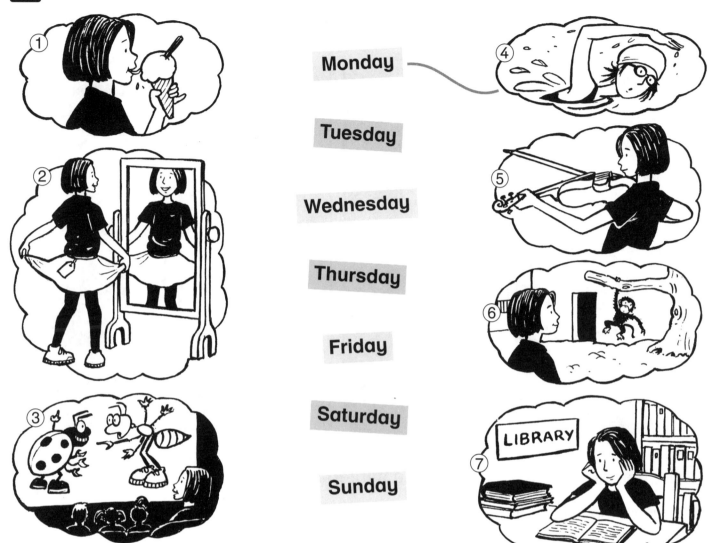

Monday
Tuesday
Wednesday
Thursday
Friday
Saturday
Sunday

3 **Choose and write.**

had	went	saw	played	bought

1 On Monday she _____ swimming.

2 On Tuesday she _____ to the library.

3 On Wednesday she _____ a film at the cinema.

4 On Thursday she _____ to the zoo.

5 On Friday she _____ the violin.

6 On Saturday she _____ a new skirt.

7 On Sunday she _____ an ice cream.

1 📻 101 **Which sister? Listen and write A (Annie), B (Bella) or C (Cathy).**

2 **Look at Activity 1. Correct the sentences.**

1 Cathy went to the sports centre by bus.

No, she didn't. She went by car.

2 Annie had breakfast at half past six.

_____

3 Bella played tennis.

_____

4 Annie played basketball.

_____

5 Cathy had an ice cream in the cafe.

_____

6 Bella had an apple juice in the cafe.

_____

3 Write.

It	had	a swimming lesson.
The animals	were	hot and sunny.
The monkey	played	with his boat.
The tiger	went	in the park.
The elephant	had	a pizza for lunch.
The baby penguin	was	to the cafe on his skateboard.

It was

1 Choose and write.

didn't   had   took   rollerblades   sunny   saw

Dear Uncle Martin   POSTCARD
Thank you very much for the
_____ . They're brilliant!
I _____ a great birthday. It
wasn't very _____ , so we
_____ go rollerblading but
Mum _____ Polly, Jack, and me
to the cinema. We _____ a
very funny film about a monkey!
Lots of love
Greg

Martin Reece
22 Park Road
Bristol

2 Write a 'Thank you' card.

Dear _____   POSTCARD

Thank you for the _____

_____

I had a great birthday.

_____

_____

_____

_____

3 ▢102 **Listen and repeat. Then write the words in the Sound Machine.**

shoes   church   delicious   station
watch   chocolate   cheese   shirt

shirt

cheese

4 ▢103 **Listen and check with the Sound Machine.**

RHYME TIME

5 ▢104 **Say the rhyme.**

On a very hot Tuesday the children had chocolate
And then there was chocolate on trousers and skirts.
The teacher said, 'Children! Now wash your hands, please!'
And then there was chocolate all over their shirts!

Can you talk about Sir Henry? Put a ✓ or a ✗.

 Can you read and say *Yes, I did* or *No, I didn't*?

I went to school on Sunday.

This morning I had cereal for breakfast.

I played with my friends yesterday.

I saw my teacher on Saturday.

 Can you number the words in these sentences?

| She | | a | | computer game. | | new | | bought | |

| four | | to | | o'clock. | | They | | cinema | | went | | the | | at | |

| Sunday | | cold. | | On | | was | | very | | it | |

| have | | I | | toast | | didn't | | breakfast. | | for | |

Now think about your progress.

OK ◯   Good ◯   Excellent ◯

88

Unit 9 Lesson 6